CAT BREEDS

BENGALS

BY ABBY DOTY

WWW.APEXEDITIONS.COM

Copyright © 2025 by Apex Editions, Mendota Heights, MN 55120. All rights reserved. No part of this book may be reproduced or utilized in any form or by any means without written permission from the publisher.

Apex is distributed by North Star Editions:
sales@northstareditions.com | 888-417-0195

Produced for Apex by Red Line Editorial.

Photographs ©: Shutterstock Images, cover, 1, 4–5, 6, 7, 8, 10–11, 12–13, 15, 16–17, 18, 19, 20, 22–23, 24–25, 26–27, 29

Library of Congress Control Number: 2024940530

ISBN
979-8-89250-307-5 (hardcover)
979-8-89250-345-7 (paperback)
979-8-89250-420-1 (ebook pdf)
979-8-89250-383-9 (hosted ebook)

Printed in the United States of America
Mankato, MN
012025

NOTE TO PARENTS AND EDUCATORS

Apex books are designed to build literacy skills in striving readers. Exciting, high-interest content attracts and holds readers' attention. The text is carefully leveled to allow students to achieve success quickly. Additional features, such as bolded glossary words for difficult terms, help build comprehension.

TABLE OF CONTENTS

CHAPTER 1
OUTDOOR ADVENTURE 4

CHAPTER 2
FROM THE WILD 10

CHAPTER 3
ACTIVE CATS 16

CHAPTER 4
CAT CARE 22

COMPREHENSION QUESTIONS • 28
GLOSSARY • 30
TO LEARN MORE • 31
ABOUT THE AUTHOR • 31
INDEX • 32

CHAPTER 1

OUTDOOR ADVENTURE

A Bengal cat and her owner take a walk outside. The cat wears a harness and leash. She wanders down the sidewalk and smells the grass. She watches birds fly above.

Many Bengal cats learn to walk on leashes.

Suddenly, a squirrel runs across the sidewalk. The Bengal crouches low. She's ready to pounce at the squirrel. But the owner gently pulls her back.

Wild animals can spread sicknesses to cats.

Leashes help owners keep cats away from danger.

OUTDOOR DANGER

Bengals like to be outdoors. But the cats shouldn't go outside without leashes. They could be hurt by animals or cars. Or the cats could get lost.

Soon, the owner and cat return home. They play together. The owner **dangles** a feather toy on a string. The cat leaps and swats at the toy.

FAST FACT
Bengals can jump up to 8 feet (2.4 m) high.

Bengals are social cats. They can play with their owners for hours.

CHAPTER 2

FROM THE WILD

Bengals are a newer **breed** of cat. They are a cross between leopard cats and short-haired **domestic** cats. People mixed those cats in the 1960s.

Leopard cats are wild animals. They live in forests throughout Asia.

By the 1980s, people began keeping Bengals as pets. The cats looked like wild leopard cats. But they were gentler and calmer.

CHANGES

People sort Bengals into generations. Cats in the first generation have one leopard cat parent. So, these cats may still act wild. Later generations have two domestic parents. So, the cats become **tamer**.

Spots help wild cats hide in shadowy forests. People wanted pets to have this pattern.

Bengals became **popular** pets. But they are illegal in certain places. Some people think they are too wild. They don't want leopard cats mixed with pets.

FAST FACT

In some places, people need **licenses** to own Bengals.

Some places only allow later generations of Bengals. These cats tend to be gentler.

CHAPTER 3

ACTIVE CATS

Bengals have lean bodies and long legs. The cats also have lots of **muscles**. Bengals can weigh up to 15 pounds (7 kg).

A Bengal's back legs are longer than its front legs. That helps the cat run and jump.

Most Bengals have short, soft fur.

Bengals have large eyes and round ears. Most have brown fur with dark spots. But their coats come in several colors and patterns.

FAST FACT

Bengals have rose-shaped markings on their fur. The markings are called rosettes.

Many Bengals have silver coats.

Bengals are active and curious. Many enjoy exploring different rooms or climbing up high. The cats often sit near windows and look outside.

NATURAL SWIMMERS

Unlike most cats, Bengals enjoy water. The cats are good swimmers. Bengals may even may hop into showers or baths with their owners.

Bengals may try to drink or play in running water.

CHAPTER 4

CAT CARE

Bengals only need to be brushed once a week. But the cats need to exercise every day. They should have lots of time and space to move and play.

Weekly brushing helps prevent Bengals from shedding.

Owners may want to have cat trees for their Bengals to climb.

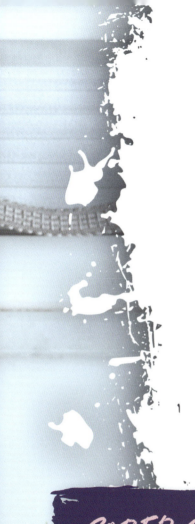

Bengals need exercise for their minds, too. Cat furniture and toys can help them stay busy. Owners can also play with the cats and teach them tricks.

BORED BENGALS

Bengals often act out when bored. Sometimes, the cats scratch and damage things. They may ruin furniture. Some Bengals may even bite or jump at people.

Bengals do best with **experienced** owners. The cats should be **socialized** from a young age. That helps the cats stay calm in new settings.

FAST FACT

Bengals may chase or hunt small animals. Owners should keep the cats away from smaller pets.

Bengals tend to be better pets for older kids and adults.

COMPREHENSION QUESTIONS

Write your answers on a separate piece of paper.

1. Write a few sentences explaining the main ideas of Chapter 2.

2. Would you like to own a Bengal cat? Why or why not?

3. How often do Bengals need to exercise?
    A. never
    B. each day
    C. each week

4. What is true of a second-generation Bengal?
    A. Both of its parents are leopard cats.
    B. One of its parents is a leopard cat.
    C. Both of its parents are domestic cats.

5. What does **pounce** mean in this book?

*The Bengal crouches low. She's ready to **pounce** at the squirrel. But the owner gently pulls her back.*

- **A.** rest
- **B.** throw
- **C.** jump

6. What does **damage** mean in this book?

*Bengals often act out when bored. Sometimes, the cats scratch and **damage** things. They may ruin furniture.*

- **A.** softly touch
- **B.** cause harm
- **C.** move around

Answer key on page 32.

GLOSSARY

breed

A specific type of cat that has its own look and abilities.

dangles

Hangs or waves above the ground.

domestic

Relating to animals that are kept by humans.

experienced

Having skills or knowledge in something as a result of doing it before.

licenses

Documents that let people do certain things.

muscles

Parts of the body that help with strength and movement.

popular

Liked by or known to many people.

socialized

Introduced a cat to new people, places, and things.

tamer

Calmer and less wild.

TO LEARN MORE

BOOKS

Jaycox, Jaclyn. *Read All About Cats*. North Mankato, MN: Capstone Publishing, 2021.

Pearson, Marie. *Cat Behavior*. Minneapolis: Abdo Publishing, 2024.

Watts, Robyn. *Clever Cats!* Sandgate, Queensland, Australia: Knowledge Books, 2024.

ONLINE RESOURCES

Visit **www.apexeditions.com** to find links and resources related to this title.

ABOUT THE AUTHOR

Abby Doty is a writer, editor, and booklover from Minnesota.

INDEX

B
breed, 10

D
domestic, 10, 12

E
exercise, 22, 25

F
feather toy, 9
fur, 18

G
generations, 12

L
leopard cats, 10, 12, 14
licenses, 14

M
muscles, 16

P
patterns, 18

R
rosettes, 19

S
squirrel, 6

T
toys, 9, 25
tricks, 25

W
water, 21

ANSWER KEY:
1. Answers will vary; 2. Answers will vary; 3. B; 4. C; 5. C; 6. B